HOW TO US

Scripture:
Write the scripture. This will help you to better focus on, retain and refer back to what you personally studied.

Observation:
Make a note of anything you specifically notice about the scripture such as, who is speaking, who is being spoken to, repeated words, italicized words.

Application:
Write out how you can apply this scripture to your life, or any revelation you've received. Where does it fit for you and/or your family? In what ways does it resonate for you personally? What do you need to do differently?

Prayer:
Journal your personal prayer for the day. Thank God for what He has shown you through His word today.

Additional Notes/Reflections:
Use this page for jotting additional study notes, putting your goals in writing, tasks you need to complete, tracking answered prayers etc.

DATE: _____

SCRIPTURE:

_____
_____
_____
_____
_____
_____

OBSERVATIONS:

_____
_____
_____
_____
_____
_____

APPLICATION:

_____
_____
_____
_____
_____
_____

PRAYER:

_____
_____
_____
_____
_____
_____

Thy word have I hid in mine heart, that I might not sin against thee. - Psalms 119:11

ADDITONAL NOTES/REFLECTIONS:

DATE: _____

SCRIPTURE:

_____
_____
_____
_____
_____
_____

OBSERVATIONS:

_____
_____
_____
_____
_____
_____

APPLICATION:

_____
_____
_____
_____
_____
_____

PRAYER:

_____
_____
_____
_____
_____
_____

Thy word have I hid in mine heart, that I might not sin against thee. - Psalms 119:11

ADDITONAL NOTES/REFLECTIONS:

DATE: _____

SCRIPTURE:

_____
_____
_____
_____
_____
_____

OBSERVATIONS:

_____
_____
_____
_____
_____
_____

APPLICATION:

_____
_____
_____
_____
_____
_____

PRAYER:

_____
_____
_____
_____
_____
_____

Thy word have I hid in mine heart, that I might not sin against thee. - Psalms 119:11

ADDITONAL NOTES/REFLECTIONS:

DATE: _____

SCRIPTURE:

_____
_____
_____
_____
_____
_____

OBSERVATIONS:

_____
_____
_____
_____
_____
_____

APPLICATION:

_____
_____
_____
_____
_____
_____

PRAYER:

_____
_____
_____
_____
_____
_____

Thy word have I hid in mine heart, that I might not sin against thee. - Psalms 119:11

ADDITONAL NOTES/REFLECTIONS:

DATE: _____

SCRIPTURE:

_____
_____
_____
_____
_____
_____

OBSERVATIONS:

_____
_____
_____
_____
_____
_____

APPLICATION:

_____
_____
_____
_____
_____
_____

PRAYER:

_____
_____
_____
_____
_____
_____

Thy word have I hid in mine heart, that I might not sin against thee. - Psalms 119:11

ADDITONAL NOTES/REFLECTIONS:

DATE: _____

SCRIPTURE:

_____
_____
_____
_____
_____
_____

OBSERVATIONS:

_____
_____
_____
_____
_____
_____

APPLICATION:

_____
_____
_____
_____
_____
_____

PRAYER:

_____
_____
_____
_____
_____
_____

Thy word have I hid in mine heart, that I might not sin against thee. - Psalms 119:11

ADDITONAL NOTES/REFLECTIONS:

DATE: _____

SCRIPTURE:

_____
_____
_____
_____
_____
_____

OBSERVATIONS:

_____
_____
_____
_____
_____
_____

APPLICATION:

_____
_____
_____
_____
_____
_____

PRAYER:

_____
_____
_____
_____
_____
_____

Thy word have I hid in mine heart, that I might not sin against thee. - Psalms 119:11

ADDITONAL NOTES/REFLECTIONS:

DATE: _____

SCRIPTURE:

_____
_____
_____
_____
_____
_____

OBSERVATIONS:

_____
_____
_____
_____
_____
_____

APPLICATION:

_____
_____
_____
_____
_____
_____

PRAYER:

_____
_____
_____
_____
_____
_____
_____

Thy word have I hid in mine heart, that I might not sin against thee. - Psalms 119:11

ADDITONAL NOTES/REFLECTIONS:

DATE: _____

SCRIPTURE:

_____
_____
_____
_____
_____
_____

OBSERVATIONS:

_____
_____
_____
_____
_____
_____

APPLICATION:

_____
_____
_____
_____
_____
_____

PRAYER:

_____
_____
_____
_____
_____
_____
_____

Thy word have I hid in mine heart, that I might not sin against thee. - Psalms 119:11

ADDITONAL NOTES/REFLECTIONS:

DATE: _____

SCRIPTURE:

_____
_____
_____
_____
_____
_____

OBSERVATIONS:

_____
_____
_____
_____
_____
_____

APPLICATION:

_____
_____
_____
_____
_____
_____

PRAYER:

_____
_____
_____
_____
_____
_____

Thy word have I hid in mine heart, that I might not sin against thee. - Psalms 119:11

ADDITONAL NOTES/REFLECTIONS:

DATE: _____

SCRIPTURE:

_____
_____
_____
_____
_____
_____

OBSERVATIONS:

_____
_____
_____
_____
_____
_____

APPLICATION:

_____
_____
_____
_____
_____
_____

PRAYER:

_____
_____
_____
_____
_____
_____
_____

Thy word have I hid in mine heart, that I might not sin against thee. - Psalms 119:11

ADDITONAL NOTES/REFLECTIONS:

DATE: _____

SCRIPTURE:

_____
_____
_____
_____
_____
_____

OBSERVATIONS:

_____
_____
_____
_____
_____
_____

APPLICATION:

_____
_____
_____
_____
_____
_____

PRAYER:

_____
_____
_____
_____
_____
_____
_____

Thy word have I hid in mine heart, that I might not sin against thee. - Psalms 119:11

ADDITONAL NOTES/REFLECTIONS:

DATE: _____

SCRIPTURE:

_____
_____
_____
_____
_____
_____

OBSERVATIONS:

_____
_____
_____
_____
_____
_____

APPLICATION:

_____
_____
_____
_____
_____
_____

PRAYER:

_____
_____
_____
_____
_____
_____

Thy word have I hid in mine heart, that I might not sin against thee. - Psalms 119:11

ADDITONAL NOTES/REFLECTIONS:

DATE: _____

SCRIPTURE:

_____
_____
_____
_____
_____
_____

OBSERVATIONS:

_____
_____
_____
_____
_____
_____

APPLICATION:

_____
_____
_____
_____
_____
_____

PRAYER:

_____
_____
_____
_____
_____
_____

Thy word have I hid in mine heart, that I might not sin against thee. - *Psalms 119:11*

ADDITONAL NOTES/REFLECTIONS:

DATE: _____

SCRIPTURE:

_____
_____
_____
_____
_____
_____

OBSERVATIONS:

_____
_____
_____
_____
_____
_____

APPLICATION:

_____
_____
_____
_____
_____
_____

PRAYER:

_____
_____
_____
_____
_____
_____

Thy word have I hid in mine heart, that I might not sin against thee. - Psalms 119:11

ADDITONAL NOTES/REFLECTIONS:

DATE: _____

SCRIPTURE:

_____
_____
_____
_____
_____
_____

OBSERVATIONS:

_____
_____
_____
_____
_____
_____

APPLICATION:

_____
_____
_____
_____
_____
_____

PRAYER:

_____
_____
_____
_____
_____
_____

Thy word have I hid in mine heart, that I might not sin against thee. - Psalms 119:11

ADDITONAL NOTES/REFLECTIONS:

DATE: _____

SCRIPTURE:

_____
_____
_____
_____
_____
_____

OBSERVATIONS:

_____
_____
_____
_____
_____
_____

APPLICATION:

_____
_____
_____
_____
_____
_____

PRAYER:

_____
_____
_____
_____
_____
_____

Thy word have I hid in mine heart, that I might not sin against thee. - Psalms 119:11

ADDITONAL NOTES/REFLECTIONS:

DATE: _____

SCRIPTURE:

_____
_____
_____
_____
_____
_____

OBSERVATIONS:

_____
_____
_____
_____
_____
_____

APPLICATION:

_____
_____
_____
_____
_____
_____

PRAYER:

_____
_____
_____
_____
_____
_____

Thy word have I hid in mine heart, that I might not sin against thee. - Psalms 119:11

ADDITONAL NOTES/REFLECTIONS:

DATE: _____

SCRIPTURE:

_____
_____
_____
_____
_____
_____

OBSERVATIONS:

_____
_____
_____
_____
_____
_____

APPLICATION:

_____
_____
_____
_____
_____
_____

PRAYER:

_____
_____
_____
_____
_____
_____

Thy word have I hid in mine heart, that I might not sin against thee. - Psalms 119:11

ADDITONAL NOTES/REFLECTIONS:

DATE: _____

SCRIPTURE:

_____
_____
_____
_____
_____
_____

OBSERVATIONS:

_____
_____
_____
_____
_____

APPLICATION:

_____
_____
_____
_____
_____

PRAYER:

_____
_____
_____
_____
_____
_____

Thy word have I hid in mine heart, that I might not sin against thee. - Psalms 119:11

ADDITONAL NOTES/REFLECTIONS:

DATE: _____

SCRIPTURE:

_____
_____
_____
_____
_____
_____

OBSERVATIONS:

_____
_____
_____
_____
_____
_____

APPLICATION:

_____
_____
_____
_____
_____
_____

PRAYER:

_____
_____
_____
_____
_____
_____

Thy word have I hid in mine heart, that I might not sin against thee. - Psalms 119:11

ADDITONAL NOTES/REFLECTIONS:

DATE: _____

SCRIPTURE:

_____
_____
_____
_____
_____
_____

OBSERVATIONS:

_____
_____
_____
_____
_____
_____

APPLICATION:

_____
_____
_____
_____
_____
_____

PRAYER:

_____
_____
_____
_____
_____
_____

Thy word have I hid in mine heart, that I might not sin against thee. - Psalms 119:11

ADDITONAL NOTES/REFLECTIONS:

DATE: _____

SCRIPTURE:

_____
_____
_____
_____
_____
_____

OBSERVATIONS:

_____
_____
_____
_____
_____
_____

APPLICATION:

_____
_____
_____
_____
_____
_____

PRAYER:

_____
_____
_____
_____
_____
_____

Thy word have I hid in mine heart, that I might not sin against thee. - Psalms 119:11

ADDITONAL NOTES/REFLECTIONS:

DATE: _____

SCRIPTURE:

_____
_____
_____
_____
_____
_____

OBSERVATIONS:

_____
_____
_____
_____
_____
_____

APPLICATION:

_____
_____
_____
_____
_____
_____

PRAYER:

_____
_____
_____
_____
_____
_____

Thy word have I hid in mine heart, that I might not sin against thee. - Psalms 119:11

ADDITONAL NOTES/REFLECTIONS:

DATE: _____

SCRIPTURE:

_____
_____
_____
_____
_____
_____

OBSERVATIONS:

_____
_____
_____
_____
_____
_____

APPLICATION:

_____
_____
_____
_____
_____
_____

PRAYER:

_____
_____
_____
_____
_____
_____

Thy word have I hid in mine heart, that I might not sin against thee. - Psalms 119:11

ADDITONAL NOTES/REFLECTIONS:

DATE: _____

SCRIPTURE:

_____
_____
_____
_____
_____
_____

OBSERVATIONS:

_____
_____
_____
_____
_____
_____

APPLICATION:

_____
_____
_____
_____
_____
_____

PRAYER:

_____
_____
_____
_____
_____
_____

Thy word have I hid in mine heart, that I might not sin against thee. - Psalms 119:11

ADDITONAL NOTES/REFLECTIONS:

DATE: _____

SCRIPTURE:

_____
_____
_____
_____
_____
_____

OBSERVATIONS:

_____
_____
_____
_____
_____
_____

APPLICATION:

_____
_____
_____
_____
_____
_____

PRAYER:

_____
_____
_____
_____
_____
_____
_____

Thy word have I hid in mine heart, that I might not sin against thee. - Psalms 119:11

ADDITONAL NOTES/REFLECTIONS:

DATE: _____

SCRIPTURE:

_____
_____
_____
_____
_____
_____

OBSERVATIONS:

_____
_____
_____
_____
_____
_____

APPLICATION:

_____
_____
_____
_____
_____
_____

PRAYER:

_____
_____
_____
_____
_____
_____

Thy word have I hid in mine heart, that I might not sin against thee. - Psalms 119:11

ADDITONAL NOTES/REFLECTIONS:

DATE: _____

SCRIPTURE:

_____
_____
_____
_____
_____
_____

OBSERVATIONS:

_____
_____
_____
_____
_____
_____

APPLICATION:

_____
_____
_____
_____
_____
_____

PRAYER:

_____
_____
_____
_____
_____
_____
_____

Thy word have I hid in mine heart, that I might not sin against thee. - Psalms 119:11

ADDITONAL NOTES/REFLECTIONS:

DATE: _____

SCRIPTURE:

_____
_____
_____
_____
_____
_____

OBSERVATIONS:

_____
_____
_____
_____
_____
_____

APPLICATION:

_____
_____
_____
_____
_____
_____

PRAYER:

_____
_____
_____
_____
_____
_____

Thy word have I hid in mine heart, that I might not sin against thee. - Psalms 119:11

ADDITONAL NOTES/REFLECTIONS:

DATE: _____

SCRIPTURE:

_____
_____
_____
_____
_____
_____

OBSERVATIONS:

_____
_____
_____
_____
_____
_____

APPLICATION:

_____
_____
_____
_____
_____
_____

PRAYER:

_____
_____
_____
_____
_____
_____

Thy word have I hid in mine heart, that I might not sin against thee. - Psalms 119:11

ADDITONAL NOTES/REFLECTIONS:

DATE: _____

SCRIPTURE:

_____
_____
_____
_____
_____
_____

OBSERVATIONS:

_____
_____
_____
_____
_____
_____

APPLICATION:

_____
_____
_____
_____
_____
_____

PRAYER:

_____
_____
_____
_____
_____
_____

Thy word have I hid in mine heart, that I might not sin against thee. - Psalms 119:11

ADDITONAL NOTES/REFLECTIONS:

DATE: _____

SCRIPTURE:

_____
_____
_____
_____
_____
_____

OBSERVATIONS:

_____
_____
_____
_____
_____
_____

APPLICATION:

_____
_____
_____
_____
_____
_____

PRAYER:

_____
_____
_____
_____
_____
_____

Thy word have I hid in mine heart, that I might not sin against thee. - Psalms 119:11

ADDITONAL NOTES/REFLECTIONS:

DATE: _____

SCRIPTURE:

_____
_____
_____
_____
_____
_____

OBSERVATIONS:

_____
_____
_____
_____
_____
_____

APPLICATION:

_____
_____
_____
_____
_____
_____

PRAYER:

_____
_____
_____
_____
_____
_____

Thy word have I hid in mine heart, that I might not sin against thee. - Psalms 119:11

ADDITONAL NOTES/REFLECTIONS:

DATE: _____

SCRIPTURE:

_____
_____
_____
_____
_____
_____

OBSERVATIONS:

_____
_____
_____
_____
_____

APPLICATION:

_____
_____
_____
_____
_____

PRAYER:

_____
_____
_____
_____
_____
_____

Thy word have I hid in mine heart, that I might not sin against thee. - Psalms 119:11

ADDITONAL NOTES/REFLECTIONS:

DATE: _____

SCRIPTURE:

_____
_____
_____
_____
_____
_____

OBSERVATIONS:

_____
_____
_____
_____
_____
_____

APPLICATION:

_____
_____
_____
_____
_____
_____

PRAYER:

_____
_____
_____
_____
_____
_____

Thy word have I hid in mine heart, that I might not sin against thee. - Psalms 119:11

ADDITONAL NOTES/REFLECTIONS:

DATE: _____

SCRIPTURE:

_____
_____
_____
_____
_____
_____

OBSERVATIONS:

_____
_____
_____
_____
_____
_____

APPLICATION:

_____
_____
_____
_____
_____
_____

PRAYER:

_____
_____
_____
_____
_____
_____

Thy word have I hid in mine heart, that I might not sin against thee. - Psalms 119:11

ADDITONAL NOTES/REFLECTIONS:

DATE: _____

SCRIPTURE:

_____
_____
_____
_____
_____
_____

OBSERVATIONS:

_____
_____
_____
_____
_____
_____

APPLICATION:

_____
_____
_____
_____
_____
_____

PRAYER:

_____
_____
_____
_____
_____
_____

Thy word have I hid in mine heart, that I might not sin against thee. - Psalms 119:11

ADDITONAL NOTES/REFLECTIONS:

DATE: _____

SCRIPTURE:

_____
_____
_____
_____
_____
_____

OBSERVATIONS:

_____
_____
_____
_____
_____
_____

APPLICATION:

_____
_____
_____
_____
_____
_____

PRAYER:

_____
_____
_____
_____
_____
_____

Thy word have I hid in mine heart, that I might not sin against thee. - Psalms 119:11

ADDITONAL NOTES/REFLECTIONS:

DATE: _____

SCRIPTURE:

_____
_____
_____
_____
_____
_____

OBSERVATIONS:

_____
_____
_____
_____
_____
_____

APPLICATION:

_____
_____
_____
_____
_____
_____

PRAYER:

_____
_____
_____
_____
_____
_____
_____

Thy word have I hid in mine heart, that I might not sin against thee. - Psalms 119:11

ADDITONAL NOTES/REFLECTIONS:

DATE: _____

SCRIPTURE:

_____
_____
_____
_____
_____
_____

OBSERVATIONS:

_____
_____
_____
_____
_____
_____

APPLICATION:

_____
_____
_____
_____
_____
_____

PRAYER:

_____
_____
_____
_____
_____
_____
_____

Thy word have I hid in mine heart, that I might not sin against thee. - Psalms 119:11

ADDITONAL NOTES/REFLECTIONS:

DATE: _____

SCRIPTURE:

_____
_____
_____
_____
_____
_____

OBSERVATIONS:

_____
_____
_____
_____
_____
_____

APPLICATION:

_____
_____
_____
_____
_____
_____

PRAYER:

_____
_____
_____
_____
_____
_____

Thy word have I hid in mine heart, that I might not sin against thee. - Psalms 119:11

ADDITONAL NOTES/REFLECTIONS:

DATE: _____

SCRIPTURE:

_____
_____
_____
_____
_____
_____

OBSERVATIONS:

_____
_____
_____
_____
_____
_____

APPLICATION:

_____
_____
_____
_____
_____
_____

PRAYER:

_____
_____
_____
_____
_____
_____

Thy word have I hid in mine heart, that I might not sin against thee. - Psalms 119:11

ADDITONAL NOTES/REFLECTIONS:

DATE: _____

SCRIPTURE:

_____
_____
_____
_____
_____
_____

OBSERVATIONS:

_____
_____
_____
_____
_____
_____

APPLICATION:

_____
_____
_____
_____
_____
_____

PRAYER:

_____
_____
_____
_____
_____
_____

Thy word have I hid in mine heart, that I might not sin against thee. - Psalms 119:11

ADDITONAL NOTES/REFLECTIONS:

DATE: _____

SCRIPTURE:

_____
_____
_____
_____
_____
_____

OBSERVATIONS:

_____
_____
_____
_____
_____
_____

APPLICATION:

_____
_____
_____
_____
_____
_____

PRAYER:

_____
_____
_____
_____
_____
_____

Thy word have I hid in mine heart, that I might not sin against thee. - Psalms 119:11

ADDITONAL NOTES/REFLECTIONS:

DATE: _____

SCRIPTURE:

_____
_____
_____
_____
_____
_____

OBSERVATIONS:

_____
_____
_____
_____
_____
_____

APPLICATION:

_____
_____
_____
_____
_____
_____

PRAYER:

_____
_____
_____
_____
_____
_____

Thy word have I hid in mine heart, that I might not sin against thee. - Psalms 119:11

ADDITONAL NOTES/REFLECTIONS:

DATE: _____

SCRIPTURE:

_____
_____
_____
_____
_____
_____

OBSERVATIONS:

_____
_____
_____
_____
_____
_____

APPLICATION:

_____
_____
_____
_____
_____
_____

PRAYER:

_____
_____
_____
_____
_____
_____

Thy word have I hid in mine heart, that I might not sin against thee. - Psalms 119:11

ADDITONAL NOTES/REFLECTIONS:

DATE: _____

SCRIPTURE:

_____
_____
_____
_____
_____
_____

OBSERVATIONS:

_____
_____
_____
_____
_____
_____

APPLICATION:

_____
_____
_____
_____
_____
_____

PRAYER:

_____
_____
_____
_____
_____
_____

Thy word have I hid in mine heart, that I might not sin against thee. - Psalms 119:11

ADDITONAL NOTES/REFLECTIONS:

DATE: _____

SCRIPTURE:

_____
_____
_____
_____
_____
_____

OBSERVATIONS:

_____
_____
_____
_____
_____

APPLICATION:

_____
_____
_____
_____
_____
_____

PRAYER:

_____
_____
_____
_____
_____
_____

Thy word have I hid in mine heart, that I might not sin against thee. - Psalms 119:11

ADDITONAL NOTES/REFLECTIONS:

DATE: _____

SCRIPTURE:

_____
_____
_____
_____
_____
_____

OBSERVATIONS:

_____
_____
_____
_____
_____
_____

APPLICATION:

_____
_____
_____
_____
_____
_____

PRAYER:

_____
_____
_____
_____
_____
_____

Thy word have I hid in mine heart, that I might not sin against thee. - Psalms 119:11

ADDITONAL NOTES/REFLECTIONS:

DATE: _____

SCRIPTURE:

_____
_____
_____
_____
_____
_____

OBSERVATIONS:

_____
_____
_____
_____
_____
_____

APPLICATION:

_____
_____
_____
_____
_____
_____

PRAYER:

_____
_____
_____
_____
_____
_____

Thy word have I hid in mine heart, that I might not sin against thee. - Psalms 119:11

ADDITONAL NOTES/REFLECTIONS:

DATE: _____

SCRIPTURE:

_____
_____
_____
_____
_____

OBSERVATIONS:

_____
_____
_____
_____
_____

APPLICATION:

_____
_____
_____
_____
_____

PRAYER:

_____
_____
_____
_____
_____

Thy word have I hid in mine heart, that I might not sin against thee. - Psalms 119:11

ADDITONAL NOTES/REFLECTIONS:

DATE: _____

SCRIPTURE:

_____
_____
_____
_____
_____
_____

OBSERVATIONS:

_____
_____
_____
_____
_____
_____

APPLICATION:

_____
_____
_____
_____
_____
_____

PRAYER:

_____
_____
_____
_____
_____
_____

Thy word have I hid in mine heart, that I might not sin against thee. - Psalms 119:11

ADDITONAL NOTES/REFLECTIONS:

DATE: _____

SCRIPTURE:

_____
_____
_____
_____
_____
_____

OBSERVATIONS:

_____
_____
_____
_____
_____
_____

APPLICATION:

_____
_____
_____
_____
_____
_____

PRAYER:

_____
_____
_____
_____
_____
_____

Thy word have I hid in mine heart, that I might not sin against thee. - Psalms 119:11

ADDITONAL NOTES/REFLECTIONS:

DATE: _____

SCRIPTURE:

_____
_____
_____
_____
_____
_____

OBSERVATIONS:

_____
_____
_____
_____
_____

APPLICATION:

_____
_____
_____
_____
_____

PRAYER:

_____
_____
_____
_____
_____

Thy word have I hid in mine heart, that I might not sin against thee. - Psalms 119:11

ADDITONAL NOTES/REFLECTIONS:

DATE: _____

SCRIPTURE:

_____
_____
_____
_____
_____
_____

OBSERVATIONS:

_____
_____
_____
_____
_____
_____

APPLICATION:

_____
_____
_____
_____
_____
_____

PRAYER:

_____
_____
_____
_____
_____
_____

Thy word have I hid in mine heart, that I might not sin against thee. - Psalms 119:11

ADDITONAL NOTES/REFLECTIONS:

DATE: _____

SCRIPTURE:

_____
_____
_____
_____
_____
_____

OBSERVATIONS:

_____
_____
_____
_____
_____
_____

APPLICATION:

_____
_____
_____
_____
_____
_____

PRAYER:

_____
_____
_____
_____
_____
_____

Thy word have I hid in mine heart, that I might not sin against thee. - Psalms 119:11

ADDITONAL NOTES/REFLECTIONS:

DATE: _____

SCRIPTURE:

_____
_____
_____
_____
_____
_____

OBSERVATIONS:

_____
_____
_____
_____
_____
_____

APPLICATION:

_____
_____
_____
_____
_____
_____

PRAYER:

_____
_____
_____
_____
_____
_____

Thy word have I hid in mine heart, that I might not sin against thee. - Psalms 119:11

ADDITONAL NOTES/REFLECTIONS:

DATE: _____

SCRIPTURE:

_____
_____
_____
_____
_____
_____

OBSERVATIONS:

_____
_____
_____
_____
_____

APPLICATION:

_____
_____
_____
_____
_____

PRAYER:

_____
_____
_____
_____
_____
_____

Thy word have I hid in mine heart, that I might not sin against thee. - Psalms 119:11

ADDITONAL NOTES/REFLECTIONS:

DATE: _____

SCRIPTURE:

_____
_____
_____
_____
_____
_____

OBSERVATIONS:

_____
_____
_____
_____
_____
_____

APPLICATION:

_____
_____
_____
_____
_____
_____

PRAYER:

_____
_____
_____
_____
_____
_____

Thy word have I hid in mine heart, that I might not sin against thee. - Psalms 119:11

ADDITONAL NOTES/REFLECTIONS:

DATE: _____

SCRIPTURE:

_____
_____
_____
_____
_____
_____

OBSERVATIONS:

_____
_____
_____
_____
_____
_____

APPLICATION:

_____
_____
_____
_____
_____
_____

PRAYER:

_____
_____
_____
_____
_____
_____

Thy word have I hid in mine heart, that I might not sin against thee. - Psalms 119:11

ADDITONAL NOTES/REFLECTIONS:

DATE: _____

SCRIPTURE:

_____
_____
_____
_____
_____
_____

OBSERVATIONS:

_____
_____
_____
_____
_____
_____

APPLICATION:

_____
_____
_____
_____
_____
_____

PRAYER:

_____
_____
_____
_____
_____
_____

Thy word have I hid in mine heart, that I might not sin against thee. - Psalms 119:11

ADDITONAL NOTES/REFLECTIONS:

DATE: _____

SCRIPTURE:

_____
_____
_____
_____
_____
_____

OBSERVATIONS:

_____
_____
_____
_____
_____
_____

APPLICATION:

_____
_____
_____
_____
_____
_____

PRAYER:

_____
_____
_____
_____
_____
_____

Thy word have I hid in mine heart, that I might not sin against thee. - Psalms 119:11

ADDITONAL NOTES/REFLECTIONS:

DATE: _____

SCRIPTURE:

_____
_____
_____
_____
_____
_____

OBSERVATIONS:

_____
_____
_____
_____
_____
_____

APPLICATION:

_____
_____
_____
_____
_____
_____

PRAYER:

_____
_____
_____
_____
_____
_____

Thy word have I hid in mine heart, that I might not sin against thee. - Psalms 119:11

ADDITONAL NOTES/REFLECTIONS:

DATE: _____

SCRIPTURE:

_____
_____
_____
_____
_____
_____

OBSERVATIONS:

_____
_____
_____
_____
_____
_____

APPLICATION:

_____
_____
_____
_____
_____
_____

PRAYER:

_____
_____
_____
_____
_____
_____

Thy word have I hid in mine heart, that I might not sin against thee. - Psalms 119:11

ADDITONAL NOTES/REFLECTIONS:

DATE: _____

SCRIPTURE:

_____
_____
_____
_____
_____
_____

OBSERVATIONS:

_____
_____
_____
_____
_____
_____

APPLICATION:

_____
_____
_____
_____
_____
_____

PRAYER:

_____
_____
_____
_____
_____
_____

Thy word have I hid in mine heart, that I might not sin against thee. - Psalms 119:11

ADDITONAL NOTES/REFLECTIONS:

DATE: _____

SCRIPTURE:

_____
_____
_____
_____
_____
_____

OBSERVATIONS:

_____
_____
_____
_____
_____
_____

APPLICATION:

_____
_____
_____
_____
_____
_____

PRAYER:

_____
_____
_____
_____
_____
_____

Thy word have I hid in mine heart, that I might not sin against thee. - Psalms 119:11

ADDITONAL NOTES/REFLECTIONS:

DATE: _____

SCRIPTURE:

_____
_____
_____
_____
_____
_____

OBSERVATIONS:

_____
_____
_____
_____
_____
_____

APPLICATION:

_____
_____
_____
_____
_____
_____

PRAYER:

_____
_____
_____
_____
_____
_____

Thy word have I hid in mine heart, that I might not sin against thee. - Psalms 119:11

ADDITONAL NOTES/REFLECTIONS:

DATE: _____

SCRIPTURE:

_____
_____
_____
_____
_____
_____

OBSERVATIONS:

_____
_____
_____
_____
_____
_____

APPLICATION:

_____
_____
_____
_____
_____
_____

PRAYER:

_____
_____
_____
_____
_____
_____

Thy word have I hid in mine heart, that I might not sin against thee. - Psalms 119:11

ADDITONAL NOTES/REFLECTIONS:

DATE: _____

SCRIPTURE:

_____
_____
_____
_____
_____
_____

OBSERVATIONS:

_____
_____
_____
_____
_____
_____

APPLICATION:

_____
_____
_____
_____
_____
_____

PRAYER:

_____
_____
_____
_____
_____
_____

Thy word have I hid in mine heart, that I might not sin against thee. - Psalms 119:11

ADDITONAL NOTES/REFLECTIONS:

DATE: _____

SCRIPTURE:

_____
_____
_____
_____
_____
_____

OBSERVATIONS:

_____
_____
_____
_____
_____
_____

APPLICATION:

_____
_____
_____
_____
_____
_____

PRAYER:

_____
_____
_____
_____
_____
_____

Thy word have I hid in mine heart, that I might not sin against thee. - Psalms 119:11

ADDITONAL NOTES/REFLECTIONS:

DATE: _____

SCRIPTURE:

_____
_____
_____
_____
_____
_____

OBSERVATIONS:

_____
_____
_____
_____
_____
_____

APPLICATION:

_____
_____
_____
_____
_____
_____

PRAYER:

_____
_____
_____
_____
_____
_____

Thy word have I hid in mine heart, that I might not sin against thee. - Psalms 119:11

ADDITONAL NOTES/REFLECTIONS:

DATE: _____

SCRIPTURE:

_____
_____
_____
_____
_____
_____

OBSERVATIONS:

_____
_____
_____
_____
_____
_____

APPLICATION:

_____
_____
_____
_____
_____
_____

PRAYER:

_____
_____
_____
_____
_____
_____

Thy word have I hid in mine heart, that I might not sin against thee. - Psalms 119:11

ADDITONAL NOTES/REFLECTIONS:

DATE: _____

SCRIPTURE:

_____
_____
_____
_____
_____
_____

OBSERVATIONS:

_____
_____
_____
_____
_____
_____

APPLICATION:

_____
_____
_____
_____
_____
_____

PRAYER:

_____
_____
_____
_____
_____
_____

Thy word have I hid in mine heart, that I might not sin against thee. - Psalms 119:11

ADDITONAL NOTES/REFLECTIONS:

DATE: _____

SCRIPTURE:

_____
_____
_____
_____
_____
_____

OBSERVATIONS:

_____
_____
_____
_____
_____
_____

APPLICATION:

_____
_____
_____
_____
_____
_____

PRAYER:

_____
_____
_____
_____
_____
_____

Thy word have I hid in mine heart, that I might not sin against thee. - Psalms 119:11

ADDITONAL NOTES/REFLECTIONS:

DATE: _____

SCRIPTURE:

_____
_____
_____
_____
_____
_____

OBSERVATIONS:

_____
_____
_____
_____
_____
_____

APPLICATION:

_____
_____
_____
_____
_____
_____

PRAYER:

_____
_____
_____
_____
_____
_____

Thy word have I hid in mine heart, that I might not sin against thee. - Psalms 119:11

ADDITONAL NOTES/REFLECTIONS:

DATE: _____

SCRIPTURE:

_____
_____
_____
_____
_____
_____

OBSERVATIONS:

_____
_____
_____
_____
_____
_____

APPLICATION:

_____
_____
_____
_____
_____
_____

PRAYER:

_____
_____
_____
_____
_____
_____

Thy word have I hid in mine heart, that I might not sin against thee. - Psalms 119:11

ADDITONAL NOTES/REFLECTIONS:

DATE: _____

SCRIPTURE:

_____
_____
_____
_____
_____
_____

OBSERVATIONS:

_____
_____
_____
_____
_____
_____

APPLICATION:

_____
_____
_____
_____
_____
_____

PRAYER:

_____
_____
_____
_____
_____
_____

Thy word have I hid in mine heart, that I might not sin against thee. - Psalms 119:11

ADDITONAL NOTES/REFLECTIONS:

DATE: _____

SCRIPTURE:

_____
_____
_____
_____
_____
_____

OBSERVATIONS:

_____
_____
_____
_____
_____
_____

APPLICATION:

_____
_____
_____
_____
_____
_____

PRAYER:

_____
_____
_____
_____
_____
_____

Thy word have I hid in mine heart, that I might not sin against thee. - Psalms 119:11

ADDITONAL NOTES/REFLECTIONS:

DATE: _____

SCRIPTURE:

_____
_____
_____
_____
_____
_____

OBSERVATIONS:

_____
_____
_____
_____
_____
_____

APPLICATION:

_____
_____
_____
_____
_____
_____

PRAYER:

_____
_____
_____
_____
_____
_____

Thy word have I hid in mine heart, that I might not sin against thee. - Psalms 119:11

ADDITONAL NOTES/REFLECTIONS:

DATE: _____

SCRIPTURE:

_____
_____
_____
_____
_____
_____

OBSERVATIONS:

_____
_____
_____
_____
_____
_____

APPLICATION:

_____
_____
_____
_____
_____
_____

PRAYER:

_____
_____
_____
_____
_____
_____

Thy word have I hid in mine heart, that I might not sin against thee. - Psalms 119:11

ADDITONAL NOTES/REFLECTIONS:

DATE: _____

SCRIPTURE:

_____
_____
_____
_____
_____
_____

OBSERVATIONS:

_____
_____
_____
_____
_____
_____

APPLICATION:

_____
_____
_____
_____
_____
_____

PRAYER:

_____
_____
_____
_____
_____
_____

Thy word have I hid in mine heart, that I might not sin against thee. - Psalms 119:11

ADDITONAL NOTES/REFLECTIONS:

DATE: _____

SCRIPTURE:

_____
_____
_____
_____
_____
_____

OBSERVATIONS:

_____
_____
_____
_____
_____
_____

APPLICATION:

_____
_____
_____
_____
_____
_____

PRAYER:

_____
_____
_____
_____
_____
_____

Thy word have I hid in mine heart, that I might not sin against thee. - Psalms 119:11

ADDITONAL NOTES/REFLECTIONS:

DATE: _____

SCRIPTURE:

_____
_____
_____
_____
_____
_____

OBSERVATIONS:

_____
_____
_____
_____
_____
_____

APPLICATION:

_____
_____
_____
_____
_____
_____

PRAYER:

_____
_____
_____
_____
_____
_____

Thy word have I hid in mine heart, that I might not sin against thee. - Psalms 119:11

ADDITONAL NOTES/REFLECTIONS:

DATE: _____

SCRIPTURE:

_____
_____
_____
_____
_____
_____

OBSERVATIONS:

_____
_____
_____
_____
_____
_____

APPLICATION:

_____
_____
_____
_____
_____
_____

PRAYER:

_____
_____
_____
_____
_____
_____

Thy word have I hid in mine heart, that I might not sin against thee. - Psalms 119:11

ADDITONAL NOTES/REFLECTIONS:

DATE: _____

SCRIPTURE:

_____
_____
_____
_____
_____
_____

OBSERVATIONS:

_____
_____
_____
_____
_____
_____

APPLICATION:

_____
_____
_____
_____
_____
_____

PRAYER:

_____
_____
_____
_____
_____
_____

Thy word have I hid in mine heart, that I might not sin against thee. - Psalms 119:11

ADDITONAL NOTES/REFLECTIONS:

DATE: _____

SCRIPTURE:

_____
_____
_____
_____
_____
_____

OBSERVATIONS:

_____
_____
_____
_____
_____
_____

APPLICATION:

_____
_____
_____
_____
_____
_____

PRAYER:

_____
_____
_____
_____
_____
_____

Thy word have I hid in mine heart, that I might not sin against thee. - Psalms 119:11

ADDITONAL NOTES/REFLECTIONS:

DATE: _____

SCRIPTURE:

_____
_____
_____
_____
_____
_____

OBSERVATIONS:

_____
_____
_____
_____
_____
_____

APPLICATION:

_____
_____
_____
_____
_____
_____

PRAYER:

_____
_____
_____
_____
_____
_____

Thy word have I hid in mine heart, that I might not sin against thee. - Psalms 119:11

ADDITONAL NOTES/REFLECTIONS:

DATE: _____

SCRIPTURE:

_____
_____
_____
_____
_____
_____

OBSERVATIONS:

_____
_____
_____
_____
_____
_____

APPLICATION:

_____
_____
_____
_____
_____
_____

PRAYER:

_____
_____
_____
_____
_____
_____
_____

Thy word have I hid in mine heart, that I might not sin against thee. - Psalms 119:11

ADDITONAL NOTES/REFLECTIONS:

DATE: _____

SCRIPTURE:

_____
_____
_____
_____
_____
_____

OBSERVATIONS:

_____
_____
_____
_____
_____
_____

APPLICATION:

_____
_____
_____
_____
_____
_____

PRAYER:

_____
_____
_____
_____
_____
_____

Thy word have I hid in mine heart, that I might not sin against thee. - Psalms 119:11

ADDITONAL NOTES/REFLECTIONS:

DATE: _____

SCRIPTURE:

_____
_____
_____
_____
_____
_____

OBSERVATIONS:

_____
_____
_____
_____
_____
_____

APPLICATION:

_____
_____
_____
_____
_____
_____

PRAYER:

_____
_____
_____
_____
_____
_____

Thy word have I hid in mine heart, that I might not sin against thee. - Psalms 119:11

ADDITONAL NOTES/REFLECTIONS:

DATE: _____

SCRIPTURE:

_____
_____
_____
_____
_____
_____

OBSERVATIONS:

_____
_____
_____
_____
_____
_____

APPLICATION:

_____
_____
_____
_____
_____
_____

PRAYER:

_____
_____
_____
_____
_____
_____

Thy word have I hid in mine heart, that I might not sin against thee. - Psalms 119:11

ADDITONAL NOTES/REFLECTIONS:

DATE: _____

SCRIPTURE:

_____
_____
_____
_____
_____
_____

OBSERVATIONS:

_____
_____
_____
_____
_____
_____

APPLICATION:

_____
_____
_____
_____
_____
_____

PRAYER:

_____
_____
_____
_____
_____
_____

Thy word have I hid in mine heart, that I might not sin against thee. - Psalms 119:11

ADDITONAL NOTES/REFLECTIONS:

DATE: _____

SCRIPTURE:

_____
_____
_____
_____
_____
_____

OBSERVATIONS:

_____
_____
_____
_____
_____
_____

APPLICATION:

_____
_____
_____
_____
_____
_____

PRAYER:

_____
_____
_____
_____
_____
_____

Thy word have I hid in mine heart, that I might not sin against thee. - Psalms 119:11

ADDITONAL NOTES/REFLECTIONS:

DATE: _____

SCRIPTURE:

_____
_____
_____
_____
_____
_____

OBSERVATIONS:

_____
_____
_____
_____
_____
_____

APPLICATION:

_____
_____
_____
_____
_____
_____

PRAYER:

_____
_____
_____
_____
_____
_____

Thy word have I hid in mine heart, that I might not sin against thee. - Psalms 119:11

ADDITONAL NOTES/REFLECTIONS:

DATE: _____

SCRIPTURE:

_____
_____
_____
_____
_____
_____

OBSERVATIONS:

_____
_____
_____
_____
_____
_____

APPLICATION:

_____
_____
_____
_____
_____
_____

PRAYER:

_____
_____
_____
_____
_____
_____

Thy word have I hid in mine heart, that I might not sin against thee. - Psalms 119:11

ADDITONAL NOTES/REFLECTIONS:

DATE: _____

SCRIPTURE:

_____
_____
_____
_____
_____
_____

OBSERVATIONS:

_____
_____
_____
_____
_____
_____

APPLICATION:

_____
_____
_____
_____
_____
_____

PRAYER:

_____
_____
_____
_____
_____
_____

Thy word have I hid in mine heart, that I might not sin against thee. - Psalms 119:11

ADDITONAL NOTES/REFLECTIONS:

DATE: _____

SCRIPTURE:

_____
_____
_____
_____
_____
_____

OBSERVATIONS:

_____
_____
_____
_____
_____
_____

APPLICATION:

_____
_____
_____
_____
_____
_____

PRAYER:

_____
_____
_____
_____
_____
_____

Thy word have I hid in mine heart, that I might not sin against thee. - Psalms 119:11

ADDITONAL NOTES/REFLECTIONS:

DATE: _____

SCRIPTURE:

_____
_____
_____
_____
_____
_____

OBSERVATIONS:

_____
_____
_____
_____
_____
_____

APPLICATION:

_____
_____
_____
_____
_____
_____

PRAYER:

_____
_____
_____
_____
_____
_____

Thy word have I hid in mine heart, that I might not sin against thee. - Psalms 119:11

ADDITONAL NOTES/REFLECTIONS:

DATE: _____

SCRIPTURE:

_____
_____
_____
_____
_____
_____

OBSERVATIONS:

_____
_____
_____
_____
_____
_____

APPLICATION:

_____
_____
_____
_____
_____
_____

PRAYER:

_____
_____
_____
_____
_____
_____

Thy word have I hid in mine heart, that I might not sin against thee. - Psalms 119:11

ADDITONAL NOTES/REFLECTIONS: